Immigrant Children
in New York City

by Lillian Forman

PEARSON

Scott
Foresman

Editorial Offices: Glenview, Illinois • Parsippany, New Jersey • New York, New York
Sales Offices: Needham, Massachusetts • Duluth, Georgia • Glenview, Illinois
Coppell, Texas • Ontario, California • Mesa, Arizona

Imagine a busy street in New York City one hundred years ago. Rows of five- and six-story brick buildings border the narrow streets. Fire escapes zigzag across the fronts of buildings. No trees grow here. The gutters are filled with muddy water and garbage. Not far from the gutters, a **peddler** stands with his pushcart. He calls out, asking people to buy his fruits and vegetables. Women gather around his pushcart. They don't complain about being **hustled** by the peddler; they're used to pushy salespeople. Other shoppers **elbow** their way through the crowds.

A few young children run in and out among the grown-ups, playing tag. They are excited to get out of the crowded apartments where they live. The young children do not seem to care that their clothes are shabby and too large. It is enough for them to be outside playing.

The older children look serious and busy. One boy, who might be ten years old, walks along slowly, carrying a pile of overcoats. His clothes are shabby. His eyes are sad. Perhaps he is wishing he could play tag with the younger children.

The people who lived in New York City's Lower East Side during the early 1900s were very poor. Many were **immigrants** who had just arrived from different countries in Europe.

Some quickly found homes by living with relatives. Still, the average **newcomer** had little money and could not speak English. They would have been lost without their relatives who had arrived earlier. Those relatives could give them **advice** and help them settle in their new country.

Children played anywhere they could in the crowded neighborhoods of New York's Lower East Side.

Many immigrants dreamed of coming to a country where everyone lived in **luxury**. Unfortunately, they found that New York City was much like their home villages. Wealthy New Yorkers, like the rich of Europe, lived in big mansions. But most immigrants lived in tiny apartments that reminded them of their old homes.

The immigrants worked hard to pay the rent and feed their families. Most knew they would never become rich. They hoped, however, that their children would live in comfort. And indeed, some of their children did go on to find better **circumstances** for themselves. But they often had to endure hardships before their lives improved.

In the early 1900s wealthy New Yorkers lived in huge mansions.

America offered immigrants opportunities to better themselves. One way that immigrant children could do this was by getting an education.

Most immigrant children wanted to go to school. But things stood in the way. Most immigrant parents were poor. Their children took jobs to help the family. These jobs were usually difficult and dangerous. There were night classes available for children who worked. But most children found it was too hard to stay awake and learn things in class after a long day at work.

The poorest immigrants lived in crowded, run-down neighborhoods.

Employers liked to hire children because they could pay them less than they paid grown-ups. In 1890 the number of factory workers under the age of 15 was 1.5 million. By 1900 the number rose to 1.7 million. Many of these children worked in garment factories, where they made clothes. These factories were called sweatshops because they were hot and the bosses made employees work very hard. Children who worked in sweatshops often became sick. Some machines were so dangerous to operate that children got injured when they used them.

In 1916 the United States Congress passed a law that stopped children under the age of fourteen from working in factories and children under the age of sixteen from working in mines. It also limited a child's working day to eight hours. However, the United States Supreme Court later overturned this law.

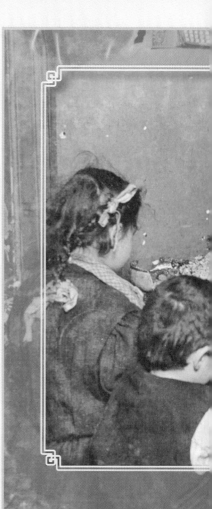

Immigrants worked long hours to make enough money to survive.

Regardless of what the laws said, most child laborers worked long hours. Then they came home to crowded apartments that were hot in the summer and cold in the winter. They and their families often had to share these small, uncomfortable spaces with lodgers. The lodgers helped pay the rent in exchange for a place to sleep. Sometimes as many as twelve people slept in one room.

Many apartments had only one window. During the summers, everyone slept on the fire escapes and roofs. Sometimes the only running water came from a faucet in the hall. All the people who lived on that floor used it.

Despite the hardships they faced, immigrant children found ways to learn and to have fun. Some did attend school, at least for a while. Once they learned to read, they were able to use New York City's public libraries.

Immigrant parents wanted their children to be educated. They also wanted them to know their heritage. So they taught them songs and told them stories from back home. They celebrated holidays and important events by cooking traditional dishes.

An immigrant family sits down to a meal.

Parents built swings, seesaws, and sandboxes in the tiny yards behind the apartments. There, mothers could watch their children to make sure they were safe. The streets of the Lower East Side, although crowded with people, became playgrounds for the immigrant children.

The East River, which flowed past the immigrant neighborhoods of the Lower East Side, was a popular spot for swimming during New York's hot summers. However, the water was extremely dirty and often caused disease.

Life for immigrants was usually difficult. Some of them struggled to change the conditions in which they and other immigrants lived. One of the most famous of these people was a man named Jacob Riis.

Riis came to New York in 1870 when he was twenty-one years old. He was shocked to see the conditions in which immigrant children lived. Riis found work as a reporter. He took pictures of poor immigrants. His photographs moved many wealthy New Yorkers to help.

In 1900, partly in response to Riis's work, New York City formed the Tenement House Commission. This group worked on plans to build comfortable, safe, and more healthy apartments. Then, in 1901, the New York State legislature passed a law to improve apartments. Apartments were made to have better fire-safety features and air shafts for more fresh air and sunlight. Indoor plumbing was also improved. The law helped stop the spread of disease. It improved the lives of New York's immigrant families.

Jacob Riis's photographs caused wealthy New Yorkers to help poor immigrant families.

The law had good effects. People made sure its rules were followed in most neighborhoods. Most of the old buildings were improved. The new ones that were built followed the law.

Still, there were too many people living in too little space. This caused problems that the law could not solve. The alleys and yards around apartment buildings were often neglected. They overflowed with garbage and dirty water. This led to the spread of diseases such as cholera, typhoid, and tuberculosis. Many of the children who played in the backyards and alleys became sick.

The Lower East Side's backyards and alleys could be unhealthy to play in.

Lillian Wald decided to do something about this. Wald was a nurse. She visited sick people in their homes on the Lower East Side. Wald believed that if she lived there herself, she could learn how to help the community.

In 1893 she opened a settlement house, or a home that reaches out to help a neighborhood, on Rivington Street. There, she and other nurses worked to improve living conditions. Then, in 1895, Wald got some of her friends to buy a large house on Henry Street. It became known as the Henry Street Settlement House.

Lillian Wald worked hard to improve life on the Lower East Side.

Wald reached out to parts of the city beyond the Lower East Side. She used money from the settlement house to hire New York City's first public school nurse. The city's Board of Education liked this idea. Nurses were hired in more schools.

By 1902 three more buildings were added to the settlement house, all on Henry Street. One of these had a gymnasium where young people could play sports. The settlement house also provided educational and cultural activities. It offered dancing lessons and held dance parties. Its pottery and painting classes gave young Lower East Siders a chance to develop their artistic talents.

That same year, Wald and the other workers opened a playground where young children could come and play. But Wald wanted to provide the children of the Lower East Side with more than just a playground. She knew that city children needed fresh air and room to run. In 1909 Wald opened two summer camps in the country for New York's immigrant children. The one for boys was called Camp Henry. The one for girls was called Echo Hill Farm.

A composer teaching music at the Henry Street Settlement House

Then, in 1915, two sisters, Alice and Irene Lewisohn, opened the Neighborhood Playhouse for the Henry Street Settlement. The theater performed plays that highlighted the culture of the Lower East Side.

Today the Neighborhood Playhouse is known as the Harry De Jur Playhouse. It still puts on plays sponsored by the Henry Street Settlement. These plays continue to reflect the culture of the surrounding community.

The mission of the Henry Street Settlement House continues. Workers there help homeless people find housing. They help parents find jobs as well as day care services for their children. A center for the arts gives classes and holds music, dance, and art festivals. And just like Lillian Wald, the people who work at the Henry Street Settlement House today make their own homes in the community they serve.

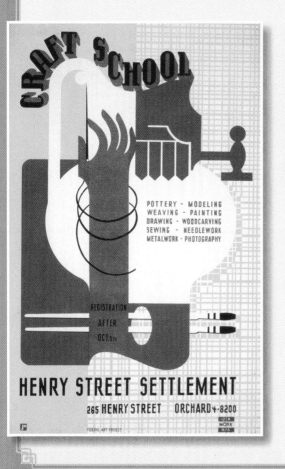

A poster telling about the Henry Street Settlement House's art program

No one **advised** Lillian Wald and the Lewisohn sisters to improve the lives of New York's immigrants. They helped people simply because they thought it was the right thing to do. However, they couldn't run the Neighborhood Playhouse and Henry Street Settlement by themselves. They needed the help of the people who lived in the neighborhood. The Henry Street Settlement House and Harry De Jur Playhouse survive today because the people they were set up to help have played a major role in keeping them running.

Glossary

advice *n.* opinion about what should be done; suggestion.

advised *v.* gave advice to.

circumstances *n.* conditions that accompany an act or event.

elbow *v.* to push with the elbows; make your way by pushing.

hustled *v.* gotten or sold in a hurried manner.

immigrants *n.* people who come into a country or region to live there.

luxury *n.* use of the best and most costly food, clothes, houses, furniture, and amusements.

newcomer *n.* someone who has just come or came not long ago.

peddler *n.* someone who travels about selling things.